Core Pre-Decodable and Decodable Takehomes

Core Pre-Decodables 1–14

Core Decodables 1–28

Grade K

Mc
Graw
Hill
Education

Bothell, WA • Chicago, IL • Columbus, OH • New York, NY

MHEonline.com

Send all inquiries to:
McGraw-Hill Education
8787 Orion Place
Columbus, OH 43240

ISBN: 978-0-07-671899-3
MHID: 0-07-671899-9

Printed in the United States of America.

6 7 8 9 QLM 20 19 18

Contents

Core Decodables

About the Core Pre-Decodable and Decodable Takehomes

The **SRA Open Court Reading** *Core Pre-Decodables* and *Decodables* allow your students to apply their knowledge of phonic elements to read simple, engaging texts. Each story supports instruction in a new phonic element and incorporates elements and words that have been learned earlier.

The students can fold and staple the pages of each *Core Pre-Decodable* and *Decodable Takehome* to make books of their own to keep and read. We suggest that you keep extra sets of the stories in your classroom for the children to reread.

How to make a Takehome

1. Tear out the pages you need.

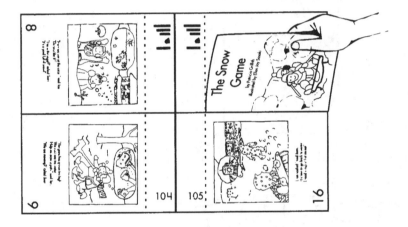

2. Place pages 4 and 5, and pages 2 and 7 faceup.

3. Place pages 4 and 5 on top of pages 2 and 7.

4. Fold along the center line.

5. Check to make sure the pages are in order.

6. Staple the pages along the fold.

Just to let you know...

A message from _____

    Help your child discover the joy of independent reading with ***SRA Open Court Reading***. From time to time your child will bring home his or her very own *Pre-Decodable* or *Decodable Takehomes* to share with you. With your help, these stories can give your child important reading practice and a joyful shared reading experience.

    You may want to set aside a few minutes every evening to read these stories together. Here are some suggestions you may find helpful:

- Do not expect your child to read each story perfectly, but concentrate on sharing the book together.
- Participate by doing some of the reading.
- Talk about the stories you read, give lots of encouragement, and watch as your child becomes more fluent throughout the year!

    Learning to read takes lots of practice. Sharing these stories is one way that your child can gain that valuable practice. Encourage your child to keep the *Pre-Decodable* or *Decodable Takehomes* in a special place. This collection will make a library of books that your child can read and reread. Take the time to listen to your child read from his or her library. Just a few moments of shared reading each day can give your child the confidence needed to excel in reading.

    Children who read every day come to think of reading as a pleasant, natural part of life. One way to inspire your child to read is to show that reading is an important part of your life by letting him or her see you reading books, magazines, newspapers, or any other materials. Another good way to show that you value reading is to share a *Pre-Decodable* or *Decodable Takehome* with your child each day.

    Successful reading experiences allow children to be proud of their newfound reading ability. Support your child with interest and enthusiasm about reading. You won't regret it!

High-Frequency Words

a	for	it	there
all	girl	little	they
am	go	look	to
and	had	of	up
as	has	on	was
at	have	out	we
be	he	said	were
boy	her	see	what
but	him	she	when
can	his	some	with
did	I	that	you
do	in	the	
down	is	then	

Sound/Spelling Correspondences in Decodables

1. /s/, /m/, /d/, /p/, /a/
2. /h/, /t/
3. /n/, /l/
4. /i/
5. /b/, /k/ spelled c
6. /o/, /r/
7. /g/
8. /j/, /f/
9. /u/, /ks/ spelled x
10. /z/ spelled z, _s
11. /w/, /k/ spelled k
12. /e/, /kw/ spelled qu
13. /y/, /v/
14. Long a spelled a_e
15. Long i spelled i, i_e
16. Long o spelled o, o_e
17. Long u spelled u_e
18. Long e spelled e, e_e
19. Review
20. Review
21. Review
22. Review
23. Review
24. Review
25. Review
26. Review
27. Review
28. Review

A Farm

by Meg Dandino
illustrated by Gary Undercuffler

Pre-Decodable 3

Mc Graw Hill Education

Bothell, WA • Chicago, IL • Columbus, OH • New York, NY

a

farm

MHEonline.com

Mc Graw Hill Education

Send all inquiries to:
McGraw-Hill Education
8787 Orion Place
Columbus, OH 43240

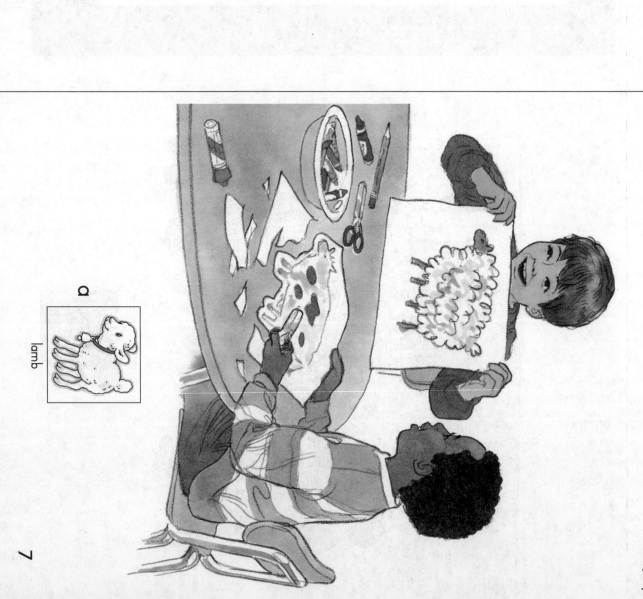

a

lamb

a

pig

a

duck

19

4

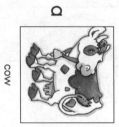

cow

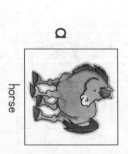

horse

5

20

The Lunch

by Lynn Edwards

illustrated by Kersti Frigell

Pre-Decodable 4

Mc Graw Hill Education

Bothell, WA • Chicago, IL • Columbus, OH • New York, NY

21

the  lunch

8

the

napkin

22

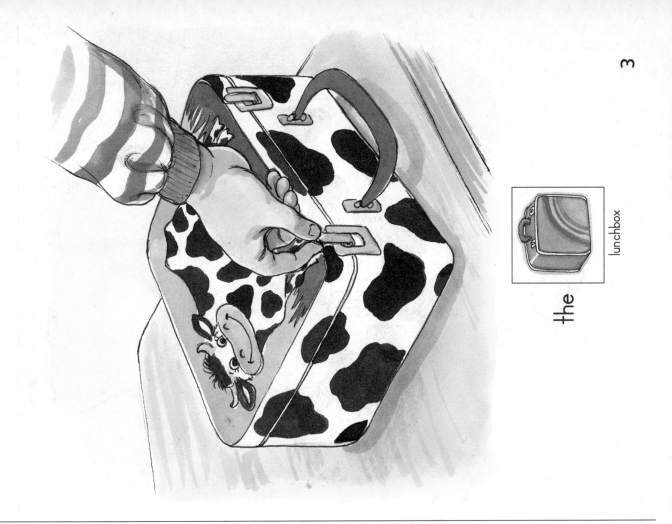

the lunchbox

the apple

the

sandwich

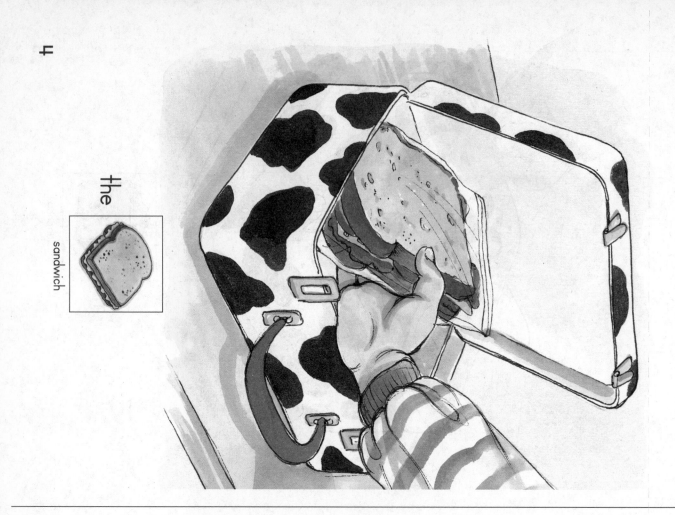

the

egg

School

by Linda Cave

illustrated by Gary Undercuffler

Pre-Decodable 5

Mc Graw Hill Education

Bothell, WA • Chicago, IL • Columbus, OH • New York, NY

the  and

school students

2

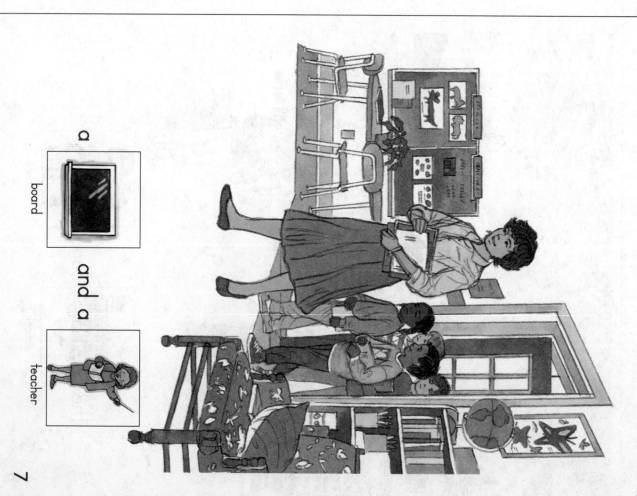

a board and a teacher

7

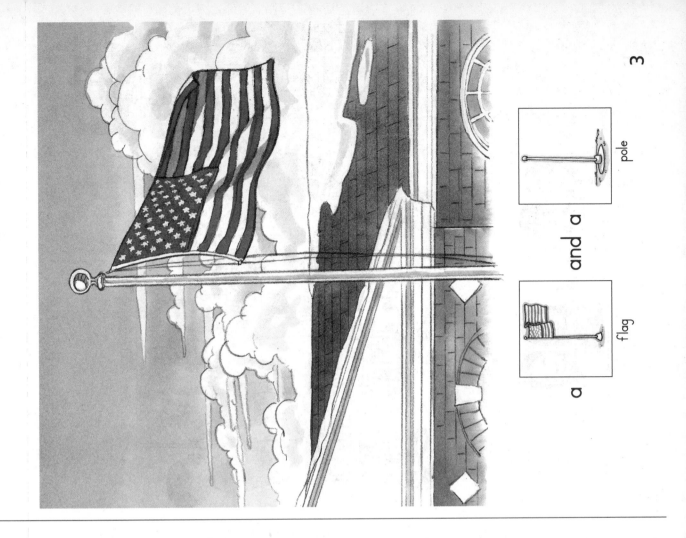

a [ ] and a [ ]

flag   pole

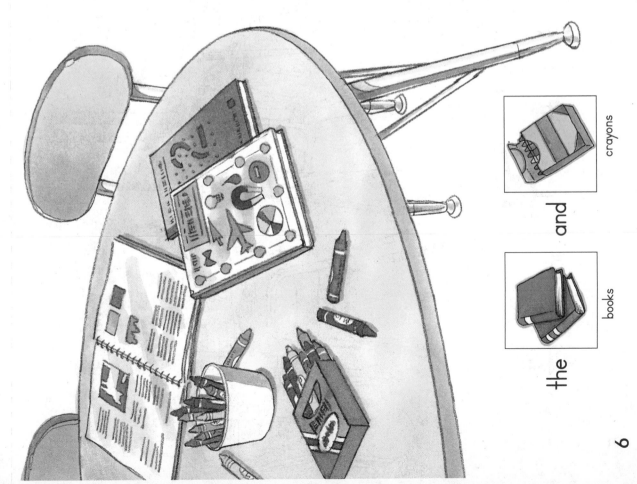

the [ ] and [ ]

books   crayons

the

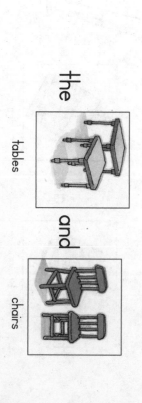

boys

and

girls

the

tables

and

chairs

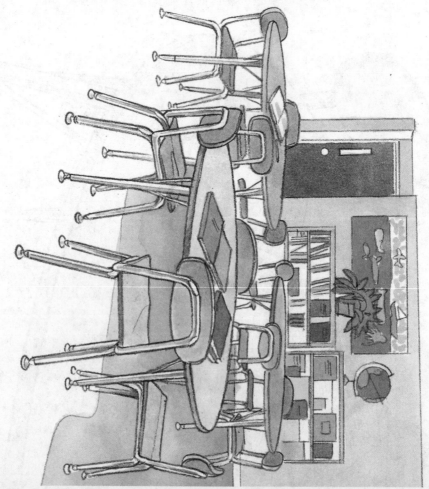

29

Go Play!

by Giulia Verzariu
illustrated by Diane Paterson

Pre-Decodable 6

Bothell, WA • Chicago, IL • Columbus, OH • New York, NY

Go  play.

8

Go a

dig   sandbox

!

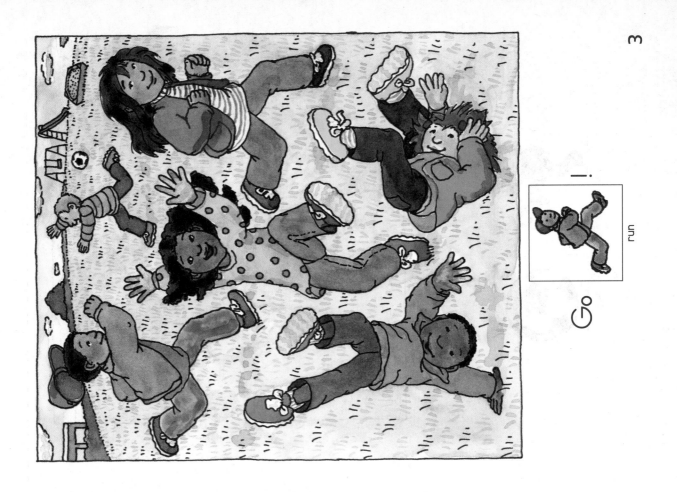

Go

run

Go down

a slide

31

Go a !

kick ball

Go a !

up swing

The  peacock had colors !

The Zoo

by Giulia Verzariu

illustrated by Diane Paterson

Pre-Decodable 7

Mc Graw Hill Education

Bothell, WA • Chicago, IL • Columbus, OH • New York, NY

2

The  owl had spots.

7

34

The had .

zoo

animals

The had .

giraffe

spots

The  had  .

zebra

stripes

4

The 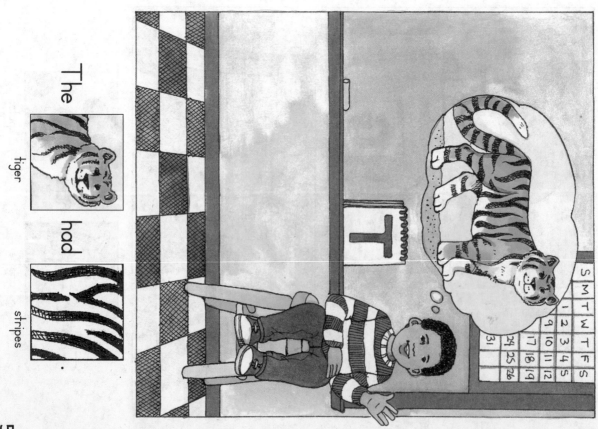 had 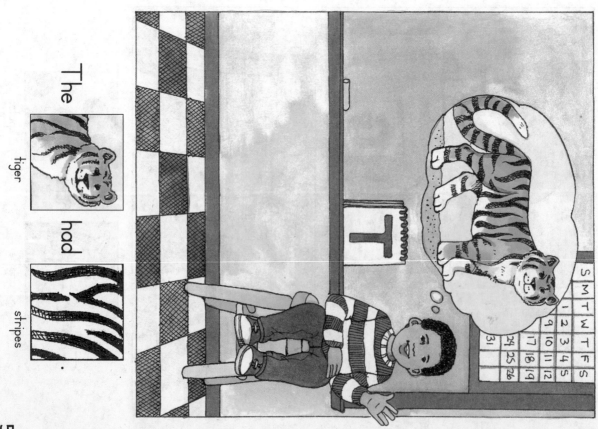 .

tiger

stripes

5

36

Colors

by Tristan Horrom

illustrated by Diane Blasius

Pre-Decodable 8

Mc Graw Hill Education

Bothell, WA • Chicago, IL • Columbus, OH • New York, NY

37

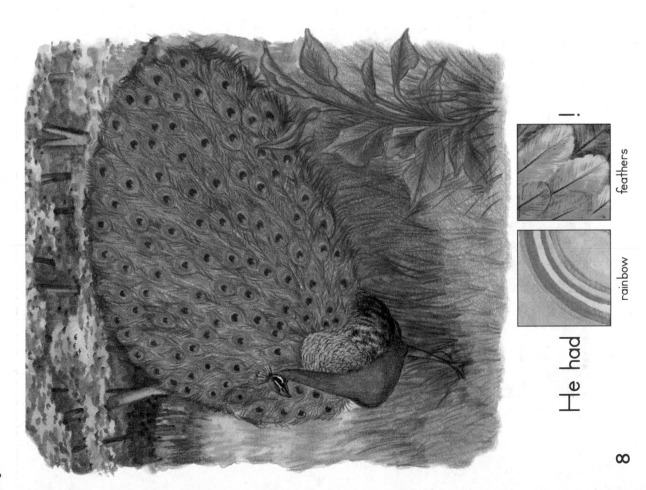

He had ▢ ▢.

rainbow   feathers

8

He had

red feathers.

He had

brown

bumps.

He had

blue

feathers.

He had

white

fur
.

He had

black

fur
.

Shapes

by Tristan Horrom
illustrated by John Hovel

Pre-Decodable 9

Mc Graw Hill Education

Bothell, WA • Chicago, IL • Columbus, OH • New York, NY

41

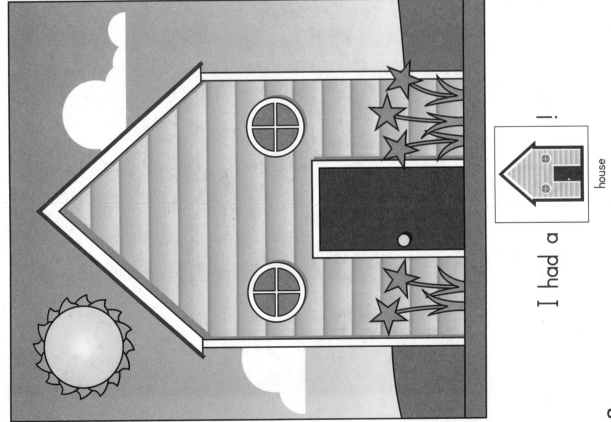

I had a ⬠!

house

8

2

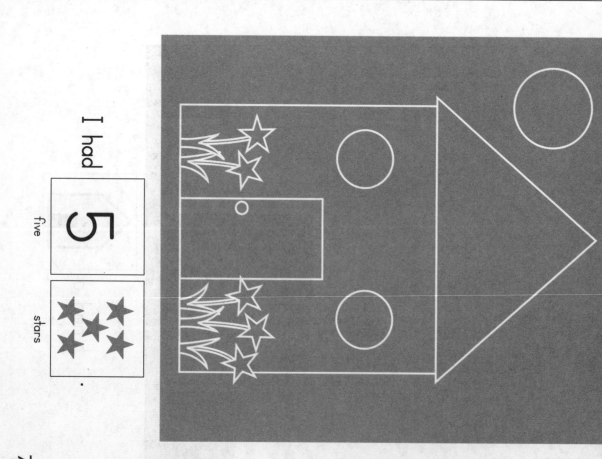

I had

5	⭐⭐⭐⭐⭐
five	stars

.

7

42

I had a [square] .

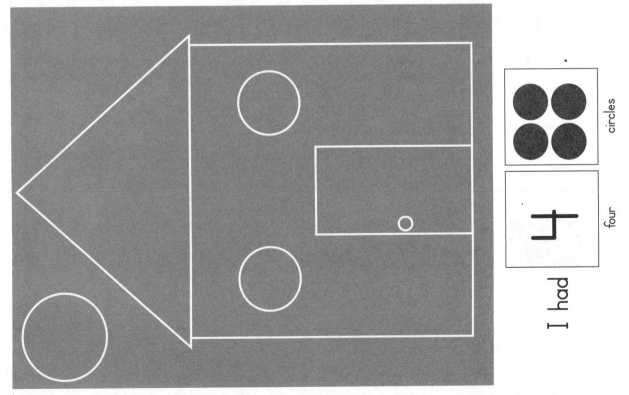

I had [4 four] [circles] .

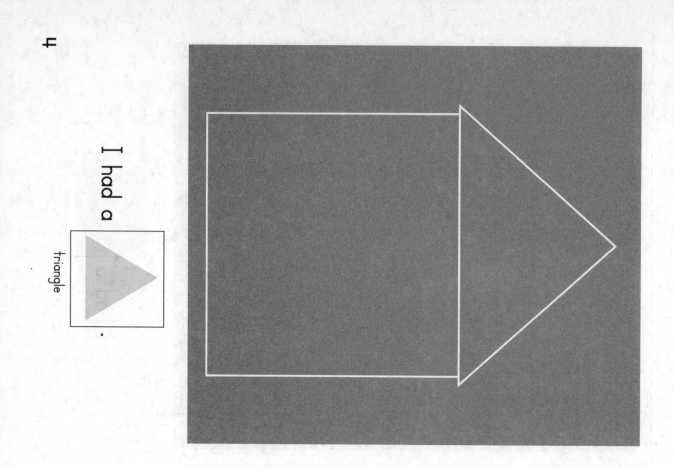

I had a _____ .

triangle

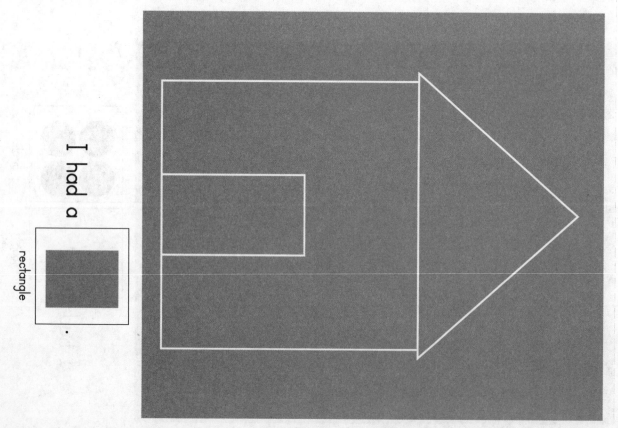

I had a _____ .

rectangle

Animal Tracks

by Sean Sanders
illustrated by Diane Blasius

Pre-Decodable 10

Mc Graw Hill Education

Bothell, WA • Chicago, IL • Columbus, OH • New York, NY

45

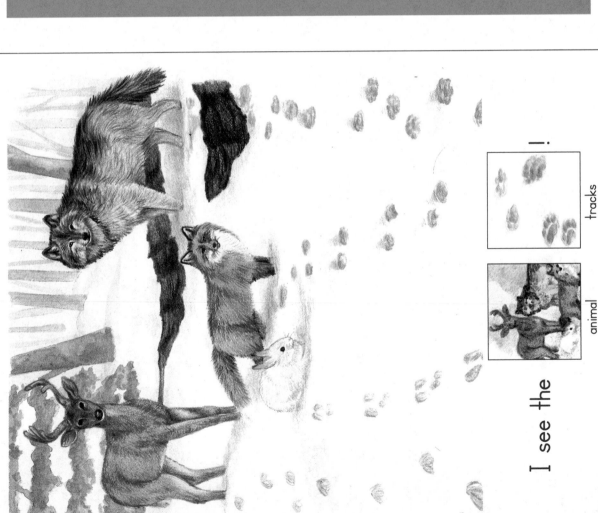

I see the animal tracks .

8

2

See the

fox

tracks

?

7

46

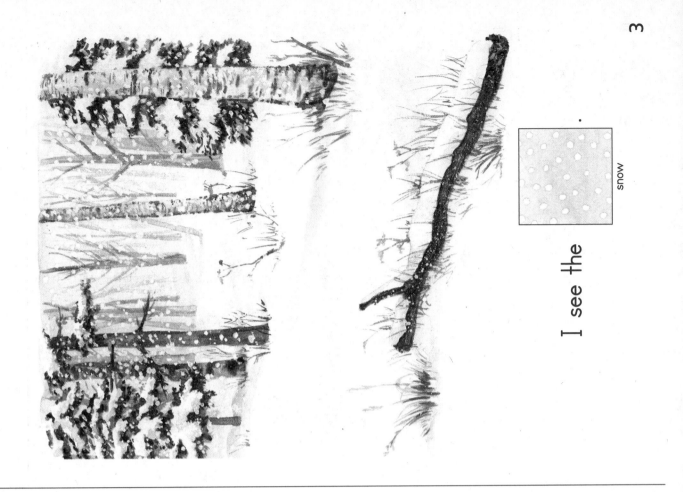

I see the ⬚ .

snow

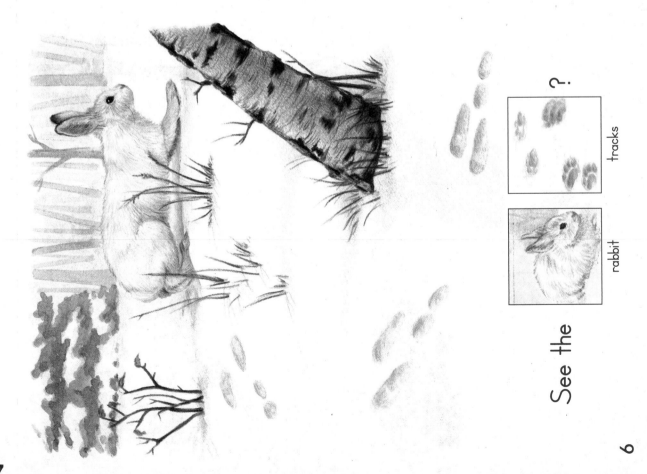

See the ⬚ ⬚ ?

rabbit   tracks

See the

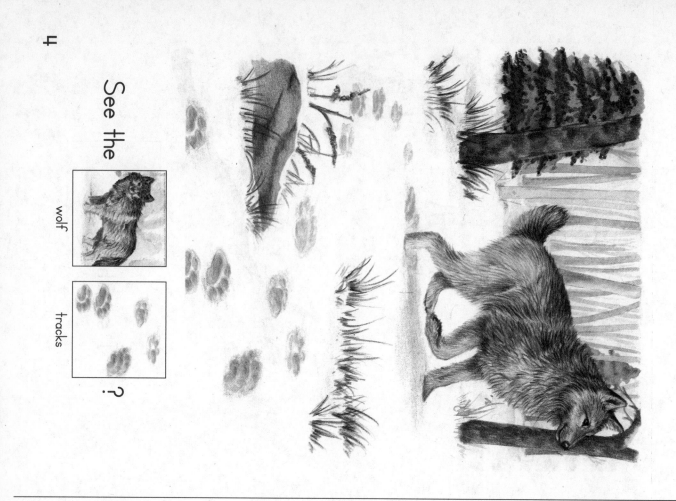

wolf tracks ?

See the

deer tracks ?

48

The Tree

by Giulia Verzariu
illustrated by Alex Wallner

Pre-Decodable 11

Mc Graw Hill Education

Bothell, WA • Chicago, IL • Columbus, OH • New York, NY

49

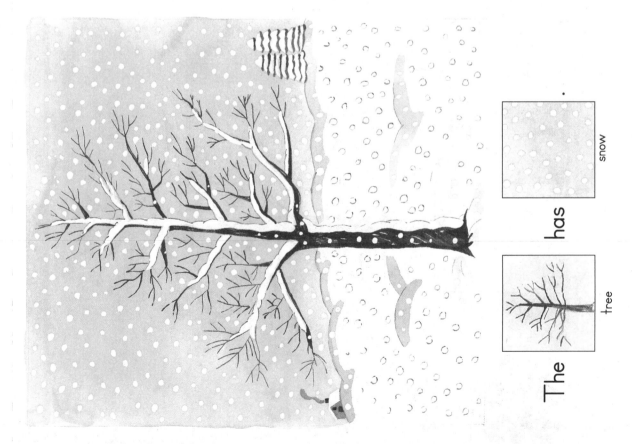

The tree has snow.

8

MHEonline.com

Send all inquiries to:
McGraw-Hill Education
8787 Orion Place
Columbus, OH 43240

The

tree

has

falling

leaves

.

The  has 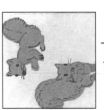 and .

tree   squirrels   leaves

6

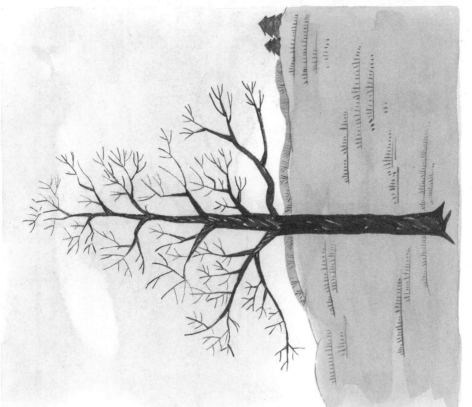

The 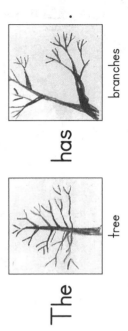 has .

tree   branches

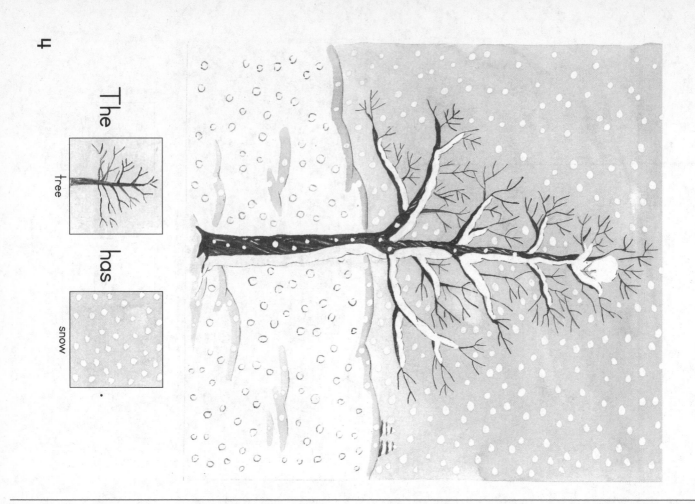

The tree has snow .

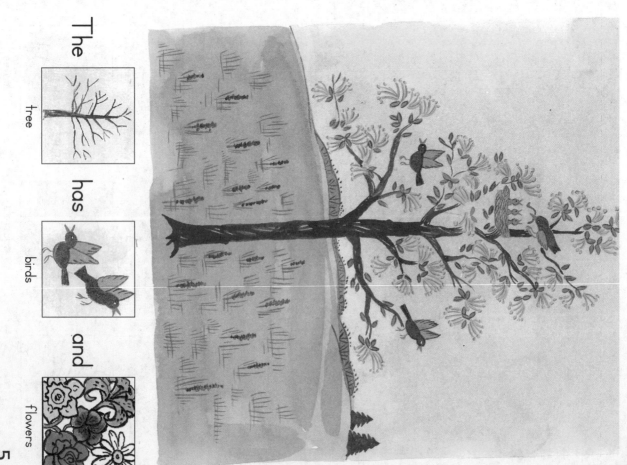

The tree has birds and flowers .

Flowers

by Giulia Verzariu
illustrated by Lorinda Cauley

Pre-Decodable 12

Mc Graw Hill Education

Bothell, WA • Chicago, IL • Columbus, OH • New York, NY

I see ___!

flowers

I see you!

53

You see

orange

flowers

You see

red   flowers

You see

purple   flowers

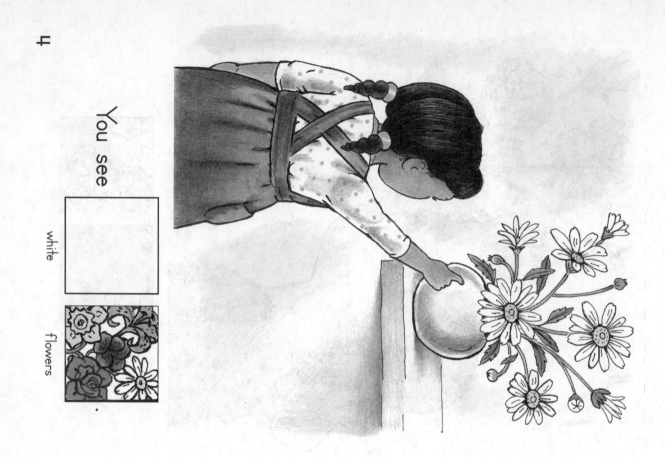

You see

white   flowers

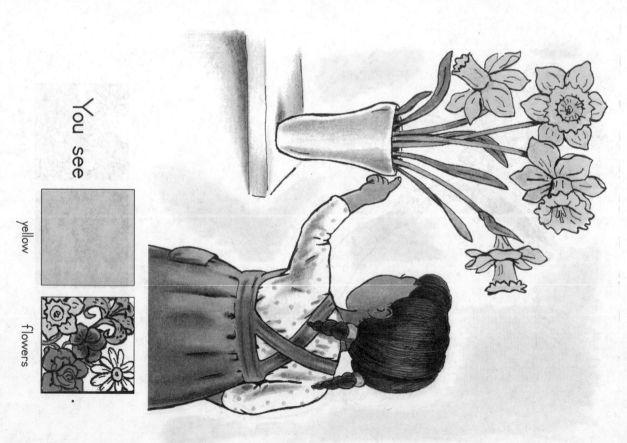

You see

yellow   flowers

We Go

by Margaret Ahn

illustrated by Meryl Henderson

Pre-Decodable 13

Mc Graw Hill Education

Bothell, WA • Chicago, IL • Columbus, OH • New York, NY

57

We go the hill

down

8

2

We go up the hill.

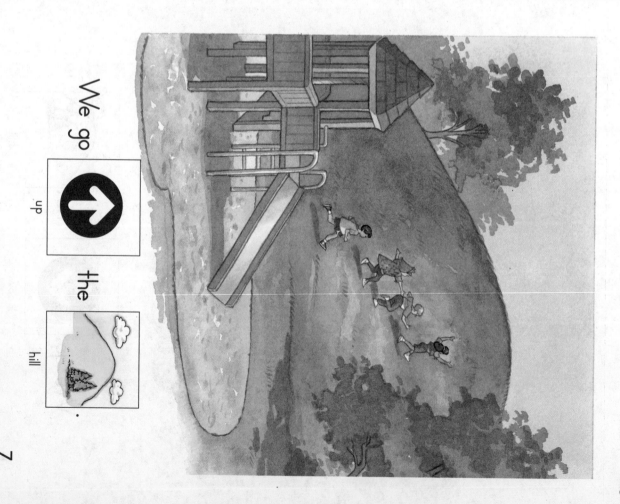

7

58

We go  the [ladder image].

up · the · ladder

We go [down arrow] the [pole image].

down · the · pole

59

3

9

We go  the .

down

slide

We go  the .

up

steps

We Carry

by Giulia Verzariu
illustrated by Tom Leonard

Pre-Decodable 14

Mc Graw Hill Education

Bothell, WA • Chicago, IL • Columbus, OH • New York, NY

61

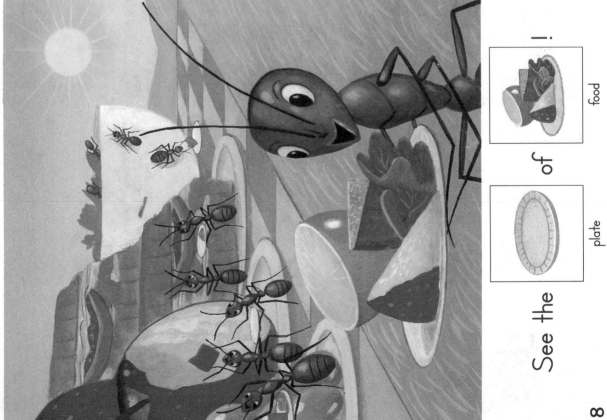

See the [plate] of [food] !

plate   food

8

We

carry

a

bowl

of

salad

.

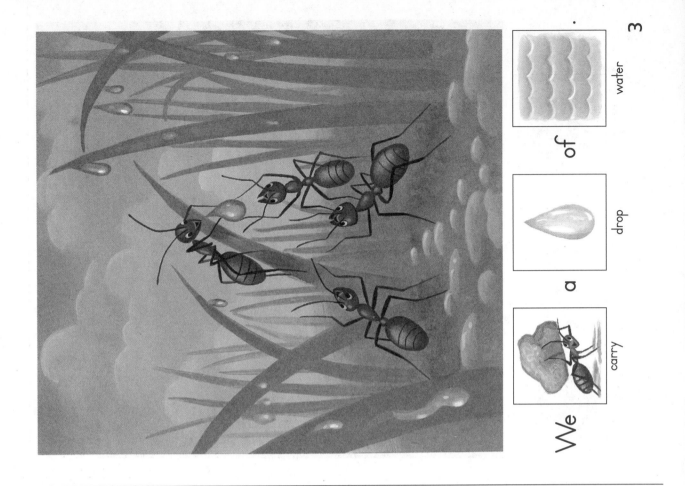

We a drop of water.

carry   drop   water

3

We  a plate of apples.

carry   plate   apples

6

We  carry a plate of sandwiches .

4

We 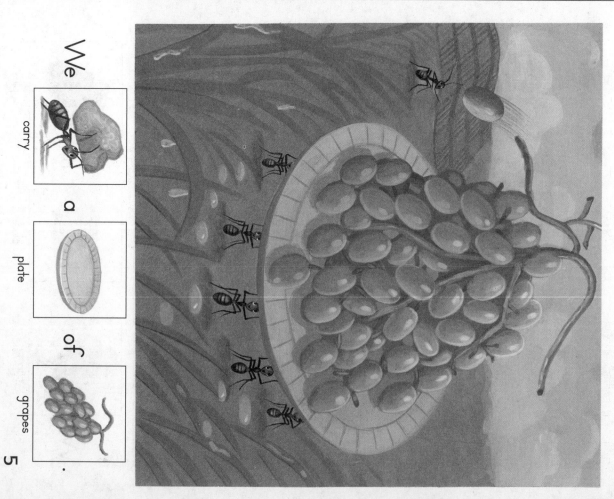 carry a plate of grapes .

5

64

Sam and Pam

by Giulia Verzariu
illustrated by Rusty Fletcher

Decodable 1

Mc Graw Hill Education

Bothell, WA • Chicago, IL • Columbus, OH • New York, NY

65

I see Pam!

8

2

I see Sam!

7

66

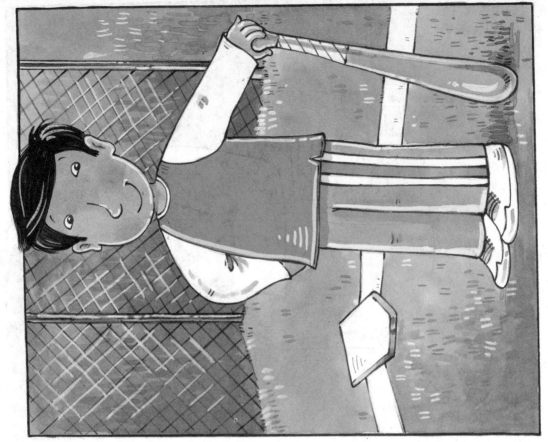

I am Sam.

I am sad.

I am sad.

I am Pam.

A Hat

by Tristan Horrom
illustrated by Yvette Banek

Decodable 2

Mc Graw Hill Education

Bothell, WA • Chicago, IL • Columbus, OH • New York, NY

69

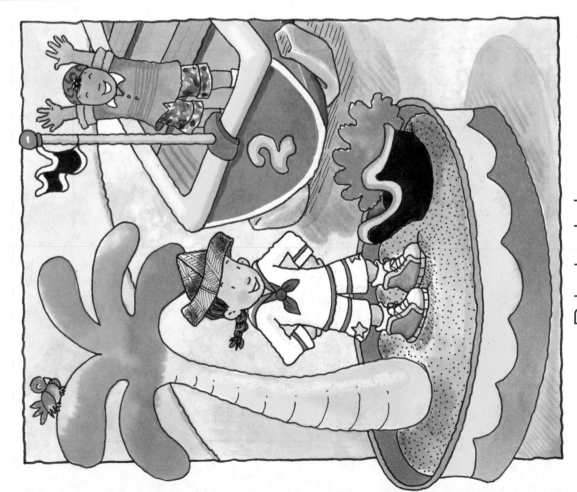

Pat at a hat

8

2

To the hat!

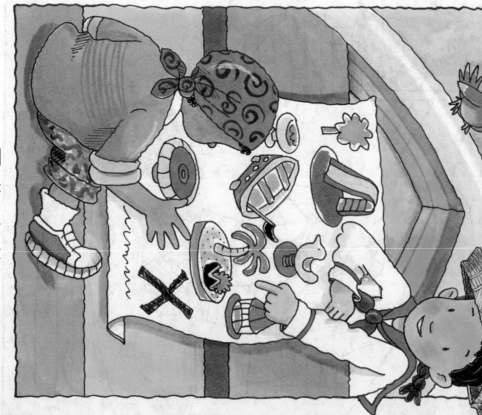

7

70

Pat, a map!

Pat taps.

6

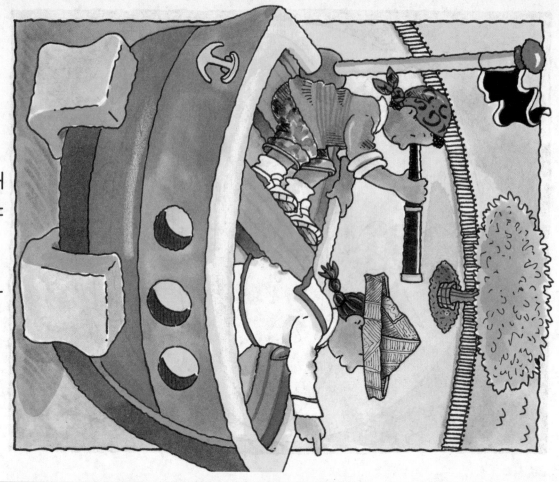

To the map!

Pat at a map

Nan and Lad

by Tristan Horrom

illustrated by Anni Matsick

Decodable 3

Bothell, WA • Chicago, IL • Columbus, OH • New York, NY

73

Damp as Lad!

8

Damp as Nan!

74

I have Nan.

Nan and Lad land.

I have Lad.

Nan naps.
Lad laps.

Tim in Sand

by Tristan Horrom
illustrated by Eva Vagreti

Decodable 4

Mc Graw Hill Education

Bothell, WA • Chicago, IL • Columbus, OH • New York, NY

Tim sits in sand!

Is Tim in sand?

It is Tim.

Tim sits.

It is sand.

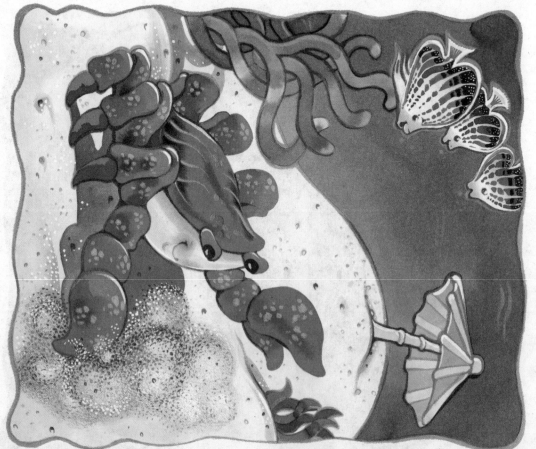

Tim hits sand.

Cal Can Bat

by Tristan Horrom
illustrated by Kate Flanagan

Decodable 5

Bothell, WA • Chicago, IL • Columbus, OH • New York, NY

81

Cal can!

Cal hit it!

8

2

Can Cal hit it?

7

82

Cal is at bat.

His pal claps.

Tim tips his cap.

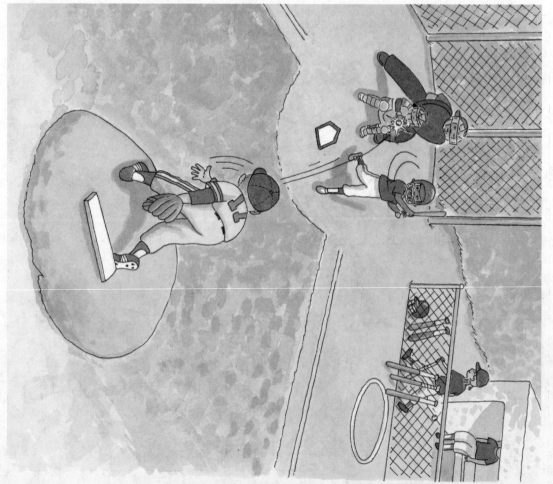

It is past Cal.

Ron Hops

by Sean Sanders
illustrated by Kate Flanagan

Decodable 6

Mc Graw Hill Education

Bothell, WA • Chicago, IL • Columbus, OH • New York, NY

85

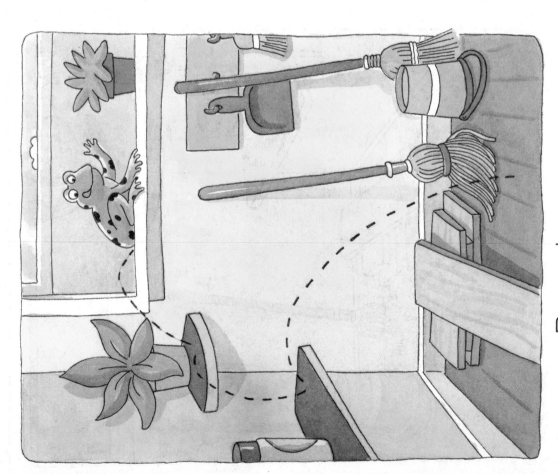

Ron can!
Ron hops on top!

8

2

Can Ron hop on top?

7

86

Ron hops on a mop.

See him plop!

See him drop!

Ron hops on a ramp.

Glad Pam

by Tristan Horrom

illustrated by Paige Keiser

Decodable 7

Bothell, WA • Chicago, IL • Columbus, OH • New York, NY

Pam did not stop.

Pam is glad!

Pam ran and got past.

The girl can sprint.

Did the girl sprint past?

Pam ran past a big dog.

Pam got past the pig.
Pam trips!

Jam Pot

by Giulia Verzariu

illustrated by Steve Henry

Decodable 8

Mc Graw Hill Education

Bothell, WA • Chicago, IL • Columbus, OH • New York, NY

93

Fran drops jam for Jim!

8

2

See the jam pot drop.

7

94

Jim, a big jam pot!

See Fran jog in fog.

Jim, grab the jam pot!

Jim flips for fig jam!

Bud and Max

by Tristan Horrom
illustrated by Laura Logan

Decodable 9

Mc Graw Hill Education

Bothell, WA • Chicago, IL • Columbus, OH • New York, NY

97

Jump on the box, Bud!

8

But the sun is not up.

Bud and Max pop up!

Bud and Max pop up!

But the sun is up.

Dig in, Max!
Dig in!

Liz and Tad

by Sean Sanders

illustrated by Ellen Joy Sasaki

Decodable 10

Mc Graw Hill Education

Bothell, WA • Chicago, IL • Columbus, OH • New York, NY

101

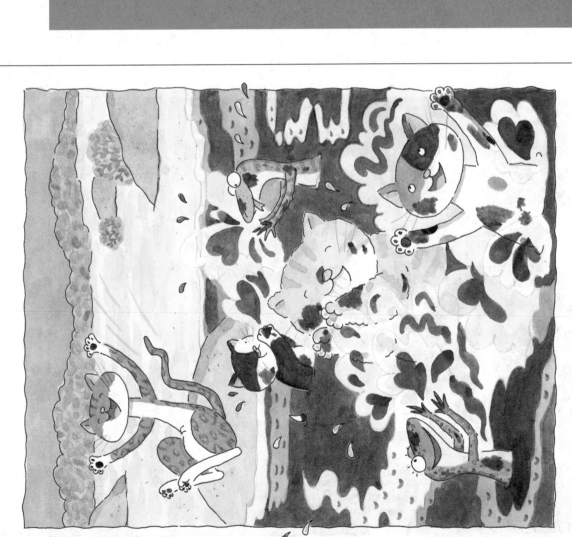

All the cats zip in.

Fun!

8

2

Liz and Tad run in the mud!

7

102

Liz and Tad nap.

Can the cats tag Liz and Tad?

All the cats run!

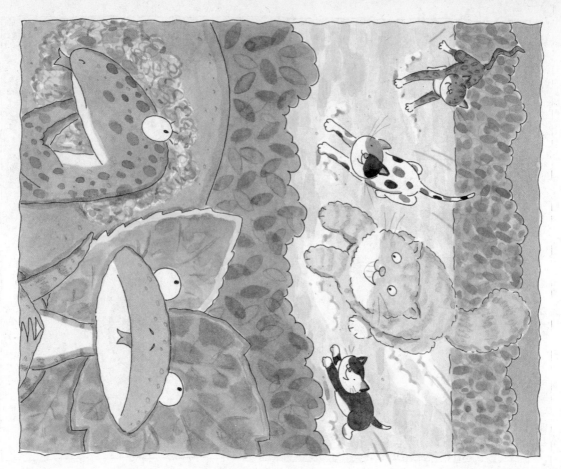

Liz zigs and Tad zags.

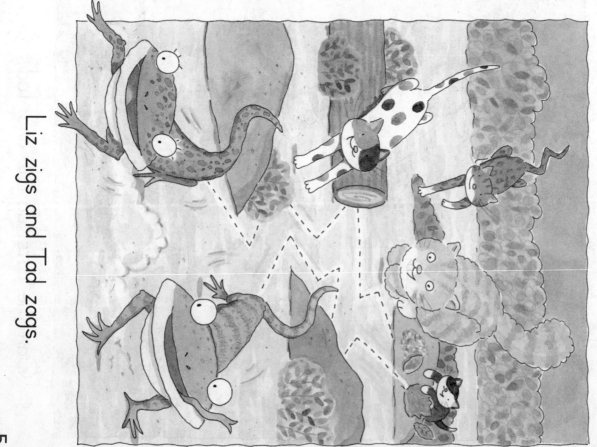

Kim and Sam

by Tristan Horrom
illustrated by Nicole In Den Bosch

Decodable 11

Mc Graw Hill Education

Bothell, WA • Chicago, IL • Columbus, OH • New York, NY

105

Kim can go fast with Sam!

8

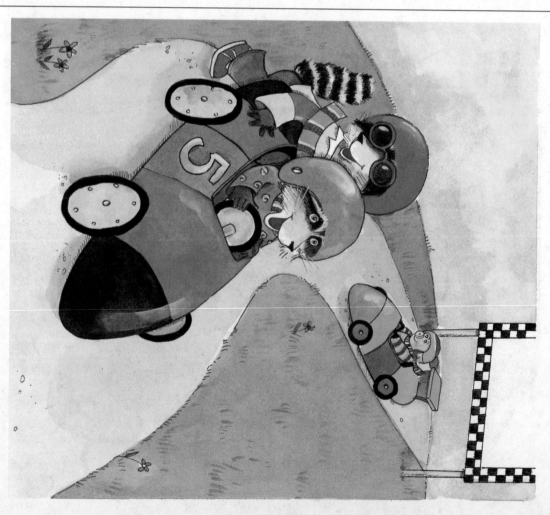

Look at Kim and Sam!

106

Kim and Sam look at a plan.

We can run it up.

We can run with a wind.

Kim and Sam can win!

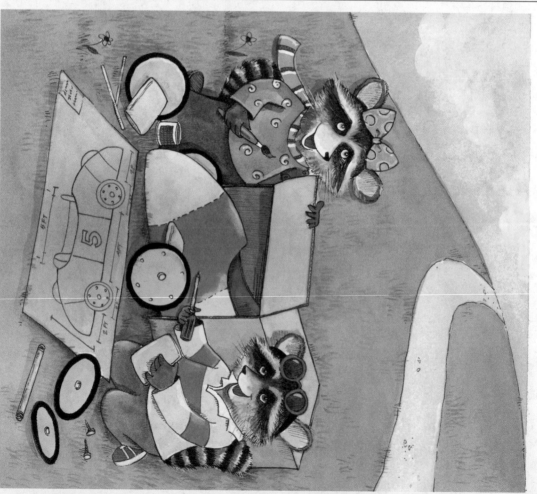

Quin and the Jets

by Tristan Horrom

illustrated by Meryl Henderson

Decodable 12

Mc Graw Hill Education

Bothell, WA • Chicago, IL • Columbus, OH • New York, NY

109

Quin helps her Jets win!

8

Send all inquiries to:
McGraw-Hill Education
8787 Orion Place
Columbus, OH 43240

Quin gets it in!
What a Jet!

110

Quin is a Jet.

3

What a step!
Can Jan stop her?

6

Quin is six.
Quin can run fast.

What pep!
Quin did not quit.

Vic Yelps

by Giulia Verzariu
illustrated by Rusty Fletcher

Decodable 13

McGraw Hill Education

Bothell, WA • Chicago, IL • Columbus, OH • New York, NY

Yes!

Vic is in the van!

Jen and Val were in mud.

7

114

Vic was in mud.
Yelp! Yelp!

Vic was not in the van yet.

115

Jen and Val were glad to help.

Get in the van, Vic.
Jump!

Jake Plants Grapes

by Tristan Horrom

illustrated by Eva Vagreti

Decodable 14

Mc Graw Hill Education

Bothell, WA • Chicago, IL • Columbus, OH • New York, NY

117

Mom and Jake ate big red grapes!

8

"Jake, can you see big red grapes?" said Mom.

118

"You can plant grapes," said Mom.

Jake did not see grapes.

"Jake, take that and dig."

"Plant that grape bud, Jake."

Mike and Spike

by Tristan Horrom
illustrated by Kate Flanagan

Decodable 15

Mc Graw Hill Education

Bothell, WA • Chicago, IL • Columbus, OH • New York, NY

121

Spike is big!

Down, Spike, down!

8

They like to ride a bike.

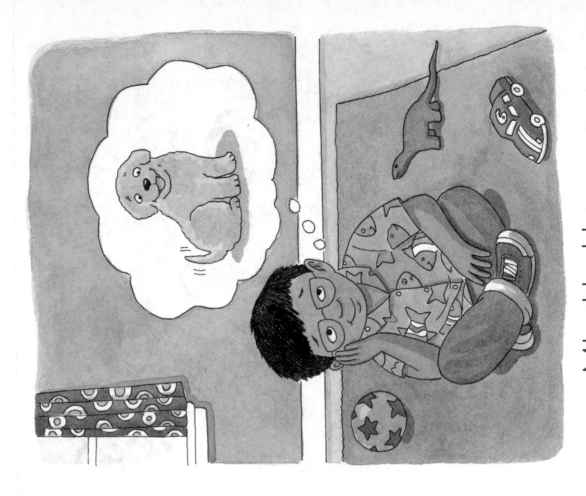

Mike did not have a pup.

They like to hike and have fun.

123

Mike is five! Mike gets Spike!

Mike and Spike hike up and down.

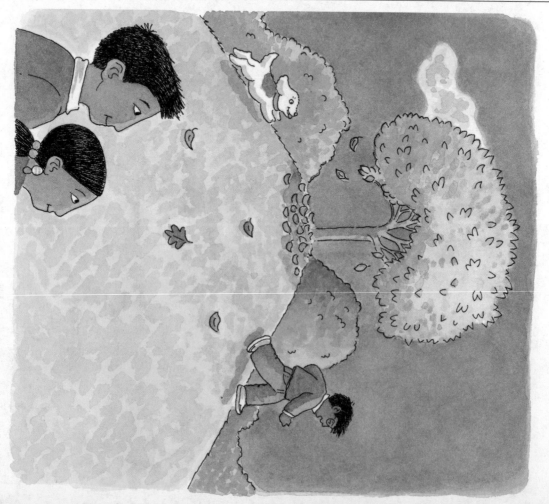

An Old Flag

by Tristan Horrom
illustrated by Jennifer Emery

Decodable 16

Bothell, WA • Chicago, IL • Columbus, OH • New York, NY

125

An old flag waves on a pole!

8

He tugs and tugs on a rope.

126

A home has a big pole.

The boy hopes he can run it up.

A boy takes out an old flag.

The flag can go out on the pole.

Cute Little Mule

by Tina Brigham
illustrated by Paige Keiser

Decodable 17

Mc Graw Hill Education

Bothell, WA • Chicago, IL • Columbus, OH • New York, NY

129

Little Mule is not hot!

They go!

8

2

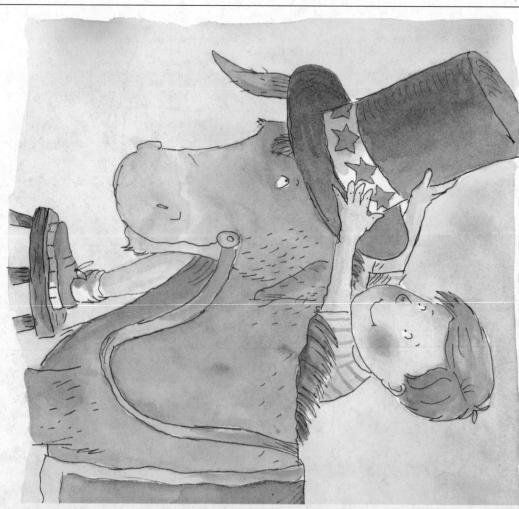

Cole has a hat.

Mule uses it.

7

130

Little Mule is cute.
Cole gets on.

Mule has an excuse—no hat!

Go, Mule, go!
I do like to ride!

They do not go.
Mule is hot.

We Did It!

by Tristan Horrom
illustrated by Laura Logan

Decodable 18

Mc Graw Hill Education

Bothell, WA • Chicago, IL • Columbus, OH • New York, NY

133

The wind takes the kite up!

We did it!

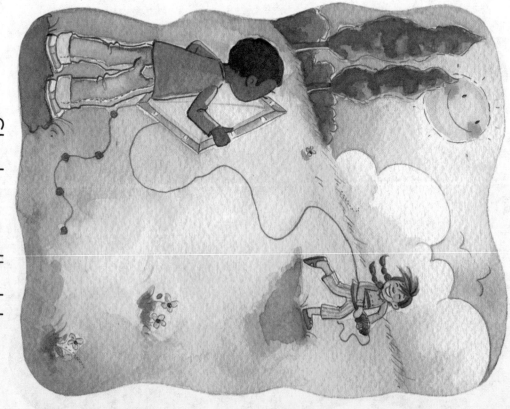

She tugs on the kite.
Run, Eve, run!

7

Eve and Pete make a kite.

Here is a rope.
Pete tapes it on.

"It can be tan," he said.

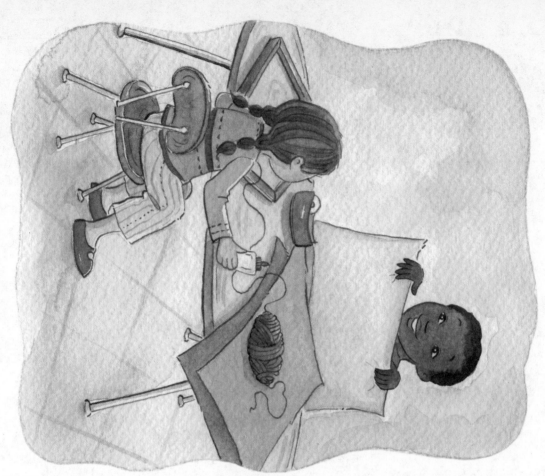

"It can be big," she said.

Steve

by Ethan Decker

illustrated by Karen Ortiz

Decodable 19

McGraw Hill Education

Bothell, WA • Chicago, IL • Columbus, OH • New York, NY

She has ten Steves!

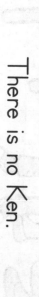

There is no Ken.
Just Steves!

Yes, Steve is here.

We see him.

But did she see Steve yet?

But there is no Ben.

Just Steves!

She has Steves!
She has nine!

She has big Steves and slim Steves.

Nat Ran

by Sofia Martinez
illustrated by Annie Pathak

Decodable 20

Mc
Graw
Hill
Education

Bothell, WA • Chicago, IL • Columbus, OH • New York, NY

141

Nat got mud on Nan and Dan!

8

2

Then Nat ran fast.
Can Dan and Nan grab him?

7

142

Mud!
Nat got in mud.

Dan had a bag.
He had rags.

So, Nan got a big, tan tub.
Then Nat hid.

Nan got a hose.
Nan made suds.

Big Meg Can Help

by Noah Williams
illustrated by Daniel Renner

Decodable 21

Bothell, WA • Chicago, IL • Columbus, OH • New York, NY

145

Big Meg can help.
Big Meg likes to help a lot.

8

When a bus has a drip, get help!

When a cab has a flat, get help!

Big Meg is glad to help.

Big Meg can help.

When a van has no gas, get help!

Wet Bandit

by Olivia White

illustrated by Sam Maldonado

Decodable 22

Mc Graw Hill Education

Bothell, WA • Chicago, IL • Columbus, OH • New York, NY

149

Jan had Bandit!

Damp Bandit was glad.

8

2

But Bandit hid and hid.

He was sad.

7

150

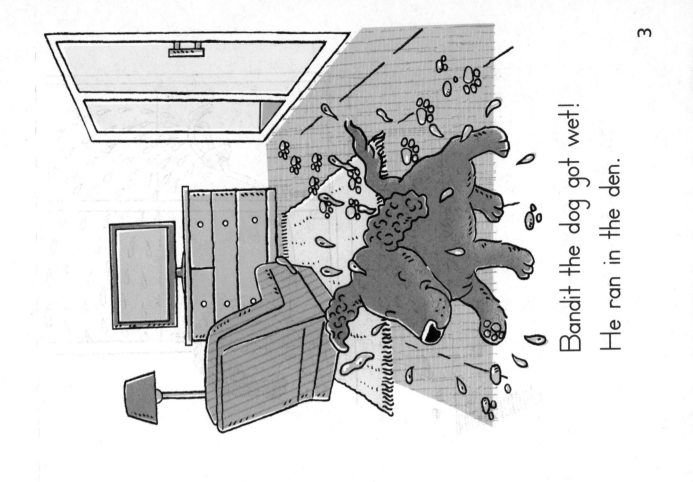

Bandit the dog got wet!

He ran in the den.

Jan spots some big, wet prints.

Can Jan get him?
Bandit left some hints.

4

Jan spots some drops.

5

152

Pine Lake

by David Sipes
illustrated by Ellie Cotton

Decodable 23

Bothell, WA • Chicago, IL • Columbus, OH • New York, NY

153

Dad said, "Time to go."

Did I mind?

No, we did lots.

8

Jim and I dig and slide.
We do not stop.

154

I am Kate.
I am on a little trip.

Hike and Bike

All of us hike.
We ride bikes to Pine Lake.

A Drive

Dad drives all of us.
Jim naps a little.

Mom said, "We can do lots at Pine Lake."

A Big Bike

by Jacob Lee
illustrated by Holly Boyd

Decodable 24

Bothell, WA • Chicago, IL • Columbus, OH • New York, NY

157

Up and down was fun.

Ron and Rose had fun.

Hope was glad.

8

2

The bike went up and down big ramps.

7

A Girl and a Bike

Hope is on a big red bike.

3

A Fun Ride

"Look, you can ride, Ron," smiled Hope.

6

The girl in red is Rose.
Rose rides with Hope a lot.

Look at Ron.
Can Ron ride?
"You can go with us," Hope told Ron.

A Box

by Max Logan
illustrated by Craig Boldman

Decodable 25

Bothell, WA • Chicago, IL • Columbus, OH • New York, NY

161

A Home

His fox likes that old box!

It can be his home.

8

2

When the boy stops, he smiles.
That box is not for him.

7

162

A Frog Box?

A boy got a box.
It can be for his frog.

They poke six holes out.
Next, they flip a wide lid.

When he gets his frog in the box, it hops out.

4

A Plan

He has a plan.
His mom can help him.

5

Jake and Quin

by Calvin Baker

illustrated by Tim O'Connor

Decodable 26

Bothell, WA • Chicago, IL • Columbus, OH • New York, NY

165

Quin can hit!

Jake claps.

Jake and Quin were fun cats!

Send all inquiries to:
McGraw-Hill Education
8787 Orion Place
Columbus, OH 43240

2

Quin uses a big bat, but he cannot hit!
Quin kept at it.

7

Quin and Jake were cute cats.
Can cats make some fun?

Fun at Bat

Jake bats.
Jake runs as Quin claps.
Then Quin bats.

Rope Fun

Quin tugs a rope as Jake tugs.
Then Jake quits.

Quin drops in some mud, but not Jake.
Jake helps Quin up.

Babe and I

by Irene Vogel
illustrated by Craig Boldman

Decodable 27

Mc Graw Hill Education

Bothell, WA • Chicago, IL • Columbus, OH • New York, NY

We have lots of fun.

I am glad.

8

169

2

Babe can even make lakes!

He just steps on land.

7

170

171

Babe Helps

I am a big, big man.
I must be ten times the size of a big van.

3

He helps me cut the logs.
We can do jobs fast.

6

A Pet Ox

I have a big pet ox named Babe.
What an ox!

Babe must be seven logs wide.
What can he do?

172

The Fox and the Grapes

by Jennifer Zimmer
illustrated by Scott Nickel

Decodable 28

Bothell, WA • Chicago, IL • Columbus, OH • New York, NY

Bad Grapes

Fox has no grapes.

"We cannot fix jam," yips Fox.

"The grapes must be bad!"

8

173

Fox zigzags and hops.

Fox yelps.

Fox cannot get the grapes!

174

Big Grapes

Fox sees big grapes up there.
Fox likes grapes.

3

Fox sees her grapes and jumps.
But she cannot get her grapes.

6

175

Fox yips, "If I can get grapes, we can fix jam. Yum!"

4

Her Grapes

Fox has a plan.
She can just jump up there.

5